HUNGAI
VIZSLA DOG:

Dog Training Book For First Time Owner

Raising Guide For Dog Owners On The Care, Diet, Grooming, Exercises & Fun, Breeding, Health, Basic Needs And More

CHARLOTTE SANDRA

Table of Contents

KEY POINT ABOUT THIS BOOK:

This book is going to supply you with a wealth of knowledge on the breed, covering topics such as its history, temperament, requirements for health and care, and more. It will also include information on the particular breed standard, which is essential knowledge for breeders to have to properly care for and breed their animals. This book on the breed will advise on the best method to train and socialize a Vizsla, as well as recommendations for preserving the dog's health and maintaining its overall well-being. Lastly, this book will include information about Vizsla rescue groups and organizations, as well as options for locating a Vizsla puppy or an adopted dog, so that readers may make informed decisions about their future pets.

CHAPTER ONE

Introduction

The Hungarian Vizsla is a dog breed that is medium-sized, beautiful, and energetic, and its hair is short, smooth, and a golden-rust color. Since they are amiable, active, and clever, they make wonderful companions, as well as household pets and watchdogs. Vizslas have a high degree of trainability and are responsive to training methods that include positive reinforcement. They are frequently employed as therapy and service dogs and thrive in activities such as agility and obedience contests. They can swim quite well, have a very good sense of smell, and they like hunting very much. They are susceptible to boredom and separation anxiety if left alone for an extended time, thus they need to lead an active lifestyle and receive lots of mental stimulation. Vizslas do best in homes where there is a lot of love and care lavished on them, and they can develop close relationships with their human families.

History And Origin

The Hungarian Vizsla is a breed of dog that has a long history that may be traced back to the 10th century. They were prized by the Hungarian tribes who lived in central Europe for their extraordinary pointing and hunting skills, which led to their domestication. During World War Two, this breed was on the verge of extinction, but a small group of devoted breeders managed to keep it alive. The Hungarian Vizsla is a popular breed of dog used today as both a companion and a sports dog.

They are well-known for their intelligence, devotion, and their enthusiasm for being around humans.

Characteristics

It has a short coat that is a golden-rust color, a strong physique and is of a size that is somewhere in the middle between small and medium. This breed is full of life and vitality, and it is devoted to its family and shows a lot of affection for them. It is well-known for its intelligence and loyalty, and it has a great desire to please those around it.

This particular breed of dog is renowned for its prowess in the field of hunting and is frequently employed both as a pointer and a retriever. The Vizsla is a wonderful addition to any household because of its kind and loving demeanor and because it makes a wonderful companion. It is also one of the breeds that is one of the easiest to teach and does not have a tendency to bark or behave aggressively. Those who are searching for an energetic, devoted, and loving companion will find that the Vizsla is the best breed for them.

Types And Differences

There are two primary varieties of the Hungarian Vizsla: those with short hair and those with wire hair.

Vizslas with short hair have a thick coat that is short and reddish-gold in color. They may have a little white blaze on the chest. Short-haired Vizslas are the most common kind. Their ears are elongated and pointed, their bodies are long and strong, and their tails are curled over their backs. Vizslas with short hair are noted for their intelligence as well as their willingness to please their owners.

Vizslas with wire-haired coats have a coat that resembles wire and is wiry and reddish-gold in color. They have a thick coat, a tail that is slung jovially over the back, and a snout that is just a tad bit longer than average. They are renowned for their keen awareness as well as their independent spirit.

Both the Hungarian and the American Vizsla are devoted,

clever, and energetic canine friends. They need a lot of physical activity, mental stimulation, and opportunities to interact with other people.

CHAPTER TWO

Reproduction

They are also recognized for their exceptional capacity for reproduction. Vizslas can have many litters of puppies during the course of a single year. Although it is not unheard of for them to have a bigger litter, their typical litter size is between six and eight puppies. They have a very short gestation period of around 63 days, and their offspring are often robust and healthy in general. The risk of congenital abnormalities being present in

Vizsla puppies is low, and these dogs are generally easy to train.

They are also famous for having exceptional mothering instincts, which makes them a perfect choice for those who have never had a dog before.

Life Expectancy

The Hungarian Vizsla dog breed is well-known for its exceptionally high life expectancy, which ranges anywhere from 12 to 15 years on average.

Size

The Hungarian Vizsla is a breed of dog that is considered to be of medium size, with an average weight range of 40-60 pounds and a height range of 21-24 inches.

Feeding

When it comes to feeding a Vizsla, it is essential to give it the correct diet that is suited to its particular requirements in this regard. The diet should include only foods of the highest possible quality that are abundant in complex carbs and protein. This breed works well on a diet that consists of both wet and dry food, with the wet food contributing between 25 and 30 percent of the total calorie intake. A variety of fresh fruits and vegetables, as well as other nutritious snacks, has to be included in the diet as well.

It is essential to provide the Vizsla with food in appropriately sized amounts several times during the day. Because this breed tended to overeat and is at ease attaining an unhealthy weight, it is essential to pay attention to how much food is provided and when it is provided to the animal. In general, for Vizsla to maintain their best possible health, they need to eat well-rounded meals at regular intervals throughout the day. It will be easier for you to keep your Vizsla happy and healthy for many years to come if you provide it with a diet that is rich in nutrients and balanced out to meet its particular dietary requirements.

Health And Common Health Issues

It is important to keep an eye out for any potential health problems associated with them.

Hip dysplasia is a prevalent health problem that affects Hungarian Vizslas. Hip dysplasia is an anomaly of the hip joint that can result in discomfort, lameness, and arthritis in the hip joint. Additional problems include progressive retinal atrophy, which is a kind of eye degeneration, and ear infections as a result of their large, floppy ears. Both of these illnesses are common in poodles. It is essential to take your Vizsla to the veterinarian regularly for exams and to discuss any concerns you may have regarding their health.

It is essential to your Vizsla's health and happiness that you provide a balanced diet, that you exercise with them regularly, and that you maintain a healthy weight for them.

Grooming

These dogs have a low maintenance level in terms of grooming since they simply require brushing once or twice a week to remove dead hair. It is important to keep up with regular nail trimming, but bathing should be reserved for when it is required. Moreover, the ears need to be examined and cleaned on a routine basis. This breed of dog is noted for having a coat that sheds very little, and it is important to keep it in excellent shape by brushing it regularly.

Training Tips And Exercise

Positive reinforcement methods, such as clicker training and reward-based training, should be utilized at the beginning of training and should continue throughout the process. It is important to provide Vizslas with lots of opportunities to interact with other canine companions, including regular walks, runs, and playtime. Kids should also have lots of opportunities for cerebral stimulation, such as via the use of interactive toys and games, to maintain their level of activity and interest.

While training a Vizsla, it is essential to have patience and be consistent with the dog's instructions. Because of this breed of dog's high level of intelligence and its rapid rate of learning, it is essential to make use of methods that involve positive reinforcement to guarantee that the dog learns the appropriate mannerisms. Maintaining a consistent approach is essential for preventing the dog from becoming frustrated or confused as a result of the training.

In addition, Vizslas should be educated in the fundamental obedience commands of sit, stay, come, and heel. Training should be done in a way that is upbeat and enjoyable for the dog so that he or she looks forward to it and has a good time with it.

Overall, the Hungarian Vizsla is a breed that is devoted, bright, and lively, and it demands a great deal of physical activity and cerebral stimulation. You can ensure that your Vizsla is content and in good health by providing it with consistent training and lots of opportunities for playing.

CHAPTER THREE

Populations

The Hungarian Vizsla is a well-liked breed of dog that is well-known for its intellect, nimbleness, and devoted nature.

The breed's adaptability and sweet demeanor have contributed to its meteoric rise in popularity around the globe.

Its hypoallergenic coat, which is also simple to care for and keep, is a key contributor to their widespread appeal.

Socialization

The Hungarian Vizsla is a breed that has to be socialized consistently since it is an energetic and social breed.

The process of socialization should begin as soon as you bring your Vizsla puppy into your house and should continue throughout the dog's whole life. It is essential to expose kids to a wide variety of people, animals, and settings in a variety of settings so that they may become well-adjusted and self-assured in any circumstance. It is essential to provide your Vizsla with the appropriate socialization if you want them to be well-mannered and pleasant.

Advantages And Disadvantages

The Hungarian Vizsla is a breed of dog that has a reputation for being extremely loyal and clever. They have a great degree of trainability and hence make wonderful companion animals. They also have a powerful sense of hunting, which makes them excellent retrievers. Because they don't need a lot of exercises, they are an excellent choice for those who live in apartments. Moreover, they are quite sociable and loving.

The Hungarian Vizsla is an energetic breed that might develop destructive tendencies if they do not get sufficient amounts of exercise and stimulation. This is one of the breed's disadvantages. They also have a propensity to speak their minds, which may be an issue in shared living areas like flats and other similar environments. Because they tend to be defiant and difficult to teach, they are not always the best breed for first-time dog owners or those who have just a little expertise with canines.

Adaptation

You should get in touch with a reliable Hungarian Vizsla breeder or look for rescue organizations in your region if you want to bring a Hungarian Vizsla into your home. It's interesting to note that Hungarian Vizslas are so intelligent that they can pick up a new command with fewer than five tries each time they hear it.

Relationship Between Owners And Other Pets

The breed of dog known as the Hungarian Vizsla is famous for the deep attachment it has with its owners. They have an unwavering commitment to their masters, are extremely loyal to them, and would do whatever in their power to make their masters happy. They are also known to be highly gregarious and friendly with other pets and animals, which makes them a fantastic addition to any household because they can get along well with other pets and animals. They have a great need to be with their owners and are more than willing to share the attention of the family with any other animals living in the home. They are known to be extremely loyal to their masters and will frequently take on the role of a watchdog for the family.

Summary

The Hungarian Vizsla is a breed of dog with a physique that is muscular despite its medium size, short coat, and temperament that is both aristocratic and sociable.

The Vizsla is a breed of dog that was originally developed in Hungary for hunting and is known for its high level of activity and enthusiasm.

Vizslas have a high level of intelligence and are easy to teach, qualities that make them wonderful companions for those who lead active lives.

Its coats may be found in a variety of hues, including sand, red, and gold. They have a reputation for being devoted and loving, and they do best living in a home environment.

The Hungarian Vizsla has the potential to be a devoted and affectionate companion for many years to come if it receives the appropriate level of care and attention.

THE END